LIONS

LIONS

A Carolrhoda Nature Watch Book

by Kathy Darling
photographs by Tara Darling-Lyon

Carolrhoda Books, Inc. / Minneapolis

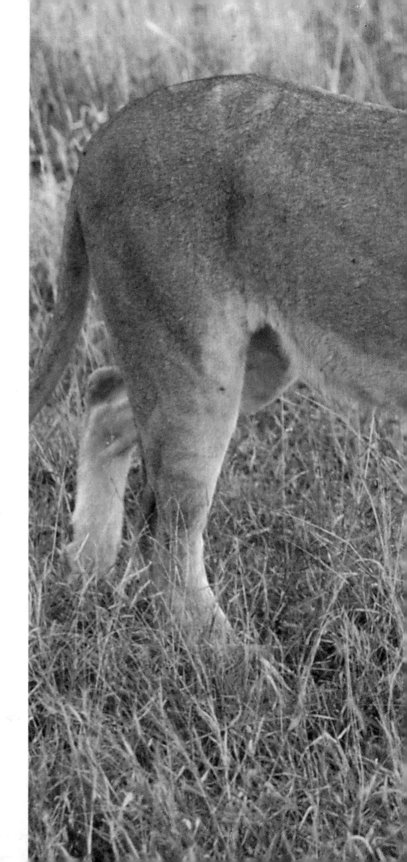

Special thanks to Michael and Norma Rattray, true conservationists. We cannot say enough good things about the work you are doing at your Mala Mala Game Reserve—and for your country of South Africa. We really appreciate the hospitality you extended to us when we visited your lion haven. Thanks also to our guide, Jaime Thorn.

The publisher would like to thank Karyl Lynn Whitman, Department of Ecology, Evolution and Behavior, University of Minnesota, for her assistance with this book.

Carolrhoda Books, Inc.
A Division of Lerner Publishing Group
241 First Avenue North, Minneapolis, MN 55401 U.S.A.

Website address: www.lernerbooks.com

LIBRARY OF CONGRESS CATALOGING-IN-PUBLICATION DATA

Darling, Kathy.
    Lions / by Kathy Darling ; photographs by Tara Darling-Lyon.
        p.   cm.
    "A Carolrhoda nature watch book"
    Includes index.
    Summary: Describes the physical characteristics and behavior of lions, as well as some of the threats they face.
    ISBN 1-57505-404-3 (alk. paper)
    1. Lions—Juvenile literature. [1. Lions.] I. Darling-Lyon, Tara, ill. II. Title. III. Series.
QL737.C23D37 2000
599.757—dc21   99-32632

Manufactured in the United States of America
1 2 3 4 5 6 – JR – 05 04 03 02 01 00

CONTENTS

BIG CATS AND SMALL CATS

Lions are scary. Meat eaters with 3-inch-long fangs, razor-sharp claws, and a 400-pound body packed with muscle are something to be scared of.

Lions are cats. They belong to a family of **mammals** called Felidae (FEE-luh-dee). The family is made up of 37 different species, or kinds, of cats. The cat body comes in many different colors and a vast range of sizes, but it is always the same basic shape.

The cat family is usually divided into four groups: big cats, small cats, cheetahs, and clouded leopards. The big cats are lions, tigers, leopards, snow leopards, and jaguars. The lion, slightly smaller than the tiger, is the second largest of the big cats.

Leopards (above) and *cheetahs (below right)* are the only cats that must compete with lions. Jaguars (far left), *tigers (below left),* and *snow leopards (bottom left)* don't live in the same parts of the world as lions do.

All cats, whether big or small, are meat eaters. They are **predators,** which means they hunt and kill other animals for food. Lions can live in forests and jungles where there are plenty of places to hide, but they prefer open grasslands with scattered trees and patches of scrubby bushes because there is more **prey** to hunt there.

8

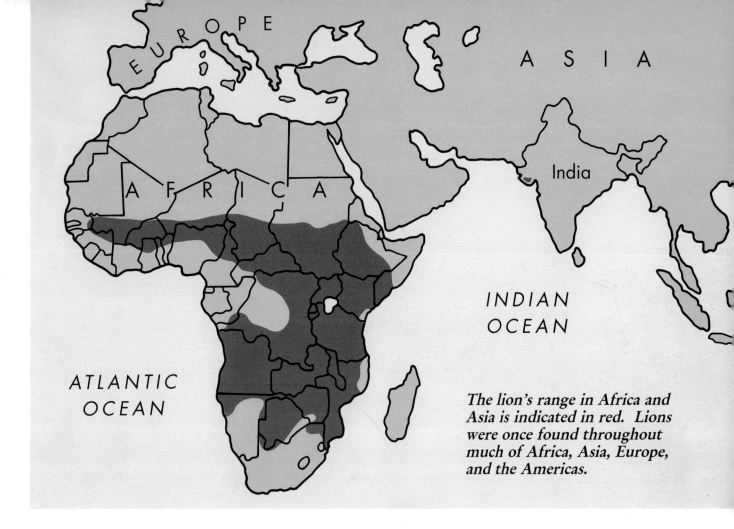

The lion's range in Africa and Asia is indicated in red. Lions were once found throughout much of Africa, Asia, Europe, and the Americas.

Few animals have been as successful as lions. Lions have ruled wherever they have lived—and they have lived almost everywhere. Lions evolved, or slowly developed, about 1 million years ago. There were many species, and the sounds of their roars were heard in Africa, Europe, Asia, and the Americas. The only continents the prehistoric lions didn't reach were Australia and Antarctica.

All of the lions became extinct, or died out, except for one species, *Panthera leo*.

The future of this last lion doesn't look very good either. The last wild lion in Europe was exterminated about 2,000 years ago. In 1900, only a dozen remained in Asia. And as the twentieth century progressed, the lion became extinct in northern Africa and was shot to protect cattle and hunted for sport throughout the rest of the continent. Thirty thousand to one hundred thousand wild lions remain in Africa and two hundred to three hundred in the Gir forest of northern India.

An adult male lion may sport a blond, red, or brown-black mane. Studies have shown that a lion with a heavy, dark mane is more attractive to lionesses than one with a blond mane.

BUILT TO KILL

Lions are the only cats in which it is easy to tell males from females. That's because males have a **mane,** or thick ruff of fur around the neck and face. Only a male at the peak of his strength has a full mane. It takes 4 or 5 years to grow. A big hairpiece, indicating a mature lion, impresses females and intimidates other males. A hairy headdress makes its owner look larger and protects his head and neck in battle.

Male lions not only look bigger than females, they *are* bigger. Standing 36 inches (91 cm) or more at the shoulder, males are several inches taller than females and often twice as heavy. A typical adult male African lion weighs at least 400 pounds (182 kg). The record setter weighed 690 pounds (313 kg). An adult female, or lioness, weighs about 280 pounds (127 kg). The lions that live in India, called Asiatic lions, are slightly smaller than African lions and the males' manes are not as full.

Because a great deal of its weight is muscle, a lion is an amazing athlete. A lion can leap across a ditch that is 30 feet wide (9 m) or over a fence that is 8 feet tall (2.4 m). And a slap from one of a male's huge front paws packs enough power to knock a zebra off its feet. A lion is not only strong, it is surprisingly speedy. Although lions can't run very far at top speed, they are capable of a 600-yard charge (550 m) at 40 miles per hour (64 km/h). Lions don't do much charging around though. They spend 20 out of every 24 hours sleeping or resting.

Creatures of tropical areas, lions have hair (a thin, single-layered coat) instead of fur (a double-layered, insulated coat). The only fur on a lion is the brown-black tuft on the end of its tail, and the mane of an adult male.

A lion's coat helps it blend into its surroundings—a definite advantage for a predator. You may think that lions are one solid color, but a close look shows that they are not the same shade all over. The hair on their backs ranges from pale yellow to light brown in color. The hair on their bellies and inside their legs is much softer, longer, and whiter. In low light, the upper part reflects starlight and the two colors merge into a solid gray, almost ghostlike color. By day, the lion's yellowish color matches the grass, which is sun-dried for most of the year.

Above: *A lion's color lets it hide in dry grass.*
Inset: *The tuft on the end of a lion's tail contains a sharp nail. Its purpose is unknown.*

A lion's primary weapons for hunting are the four **canine** teeth in its jaws. A young lion's 3-inch-long (10 cm), pointed fangs are sharp and creamy white. As the animal ages, the canines wear down and become yellow. The fangs make deep stab wounds. In the front of a lion's mouth, between the fangs, are smaller teeth used to pluck fur or feathers off skin and rip bits of meat from bone.

Lions don't have grinding teeth like the molars at the back of a human's mouth. Strict **carnivores,** or meat eaters, like cats don't need them. Lions can digest meat so easily that they don't have to chew their food. If they can swallow it, they can digest it. Chunks of flesh that are too large to swallow are cut into bite-sized pieces with the lion's large side teeth, called **carnassials.** As sharp as knife blades, the top and bottom carnassials work together like a pair of scissors. To use these meat slicers, a lion must turn its head sideways.

The upper surface of a lion's tongue is covered with hard, spiny **papillae.** These tiny, backward-pointing hooks help remove meat from bones. The tongue is as rough as sandpaper. A lion could draw blood just by licking your skin.

A lion's front teeth form a straight line rather than a semicircle (above). *This helps lions remove meat from bones* (below).

Lions are armed with 18 more tools for hunting. Each of its toes (5 on each forepaw and 4 on each hind one) has a sharp, curved claw. When not needed, these weapons are tucked away in soft, padded paws to keep them from becoming dulled. A lion's claws grow like a human's fingernails. In fact, they are made of the same substance, **keratin.** To sharpen its claws, a lion scratches them on a tree trunk.

In hunting, the claws on the forepaws grab and hold the lion's prey. They also slash through the prey's skin and muscle. The hind claws dig into the ground and anchor the lion as it goes for the kill with its teeth.

Scratching on a tree helps a lion keep its claws sharp.

Lions have round pupils instead of narrow slits like the small cat species do. A lion's eyes are always a gold color.

A lion's senses of sight, hearing, and smell are important to its success as a hunter. No animal's eyes can operate in total darkness, but a lion can see very well in low-light conditions—about six times better than a human. One reason for this is the large size of a lion's yellow eyes. Another is the **tapetum lucidum,** a lining of reflective cells at the back of its eyes. This lining acts like a mirror and directs light back across the vision cells, giving them a second chance to absorb it. The eyes of animals with a tapetum lucidum seem to glow when light is shined on them.

A lion's hearing is very keen. The cats can detect pitches both above and below the range of human hearing. They can also hear noises that aren't loud enough for us to detect. A lion's large, round ears can be turned in different directions to identify the location of a sound.

A cat's sense of smell is not as keen as a dog's or hyena's, but it is good enough for a lion to follow a scent trail to a wounded animal.

LION SOCIETY

Most cats live and hunt alone. Lions—especially lionesses—share. An adult lioness can hunt for herself, but she can't protect a hunting **territory,** or area in which she lives. Without a home containing a steady supply of food, she can't raise **cubs,** or baby lions. So a family of lionesses bands together into a **pride** and keeps other female lions off their land.

A pride is a sisterhood of closely related lionesses. The territory of a pride is passed from one generation of females to the next. Unless the pride grows too large, forcing some members to leave, a lioness remains in her birth pride all her life. Prides are closed clubs and a stranger usually has no chance of becoming a member.

Pride members rest close together, often touching each other.

The size of a pride's territory varies from 8 to 275 square miles (21–712 sq km), depending on the food it contains. A territory must also have water, good resting places, lookout positions, and safe spots to give birth to cubs.

Prides have no leaders. The lionesses are all equal members of the team. Except for fights over food, life in the pride is peaceful. The pride is a supportive family and membership has advantages. If she is injured or too old and can't hunt, a lioness is allowed to eat at kills made by her sisters once the other lionesses have eaten their share.

There are two types of prides: one has a fixed territory and lives in it year-round; the other follows prey animals that migrate, or move from one area to another. Migrating prides tend to have many members.

On open grasslands where food is plentiful, a pride typically consists of 5 to 7 adult females and their offspring. If the pride grows too large (about 30 individuals), it will split. Large prides might not ever be all together in one place. The members come and go unpredictably, alone or in small hunting parties of 5 or 6. In forest areas, an average pride consists of 3 or 4 females and their cubs.

As beneficial as group life appears to be, not all lionesses live in a pride. In areas such as the Kalahari Desert, where there isn't much large game, lionesses live and hunt alone.

Lionesses do not tolerate strangers and will mark their territory to keep other females out (above). *Mutual grooming strengthens family bonds* (right).

The males in a coalition may be true brothers or just buddies.

Living near a pride of females is a group of males. The males are not related to the females and have the right to live in a pride's territory and mate with the pride females only as long as they are strong enough to keep other males out of the territory. Males may live in association with more than one group of females, splitting their time among the prides.

The groups of males, called **coalitions,** are lifelong associations. Usually the members are brothers or cousins, but they are sometimes unrelated males who have joined together. A coalition ranges from two to nine buddies, and a lion's chances of gaining control of a pride someday depend on the size of his coalition. Large coalitions are able to overpower smaller groups. A single lion, no matter how big and strong, would have little chance to take over a pride guarded by a coalition. An established lion wouldn't be able to hold his pride for long if his teammates died.

A challenge to the males in control of a pride often begins with a "staring contest." Two males sit a few feet apart, face to face, and stare at each other—for hours! One of the lions may back down, but the confrontation usually moves on to something more physical, sometimes violently physical. Battles over the right to breed account for many male deaths, which is one reason adult females outnumber adult males by a large margin, although at birth the ratio is 50/50.

A lioness approaches males with caution.

Lionesses are afraid of male lions, even members of the pride's resident coalition—and for good reason. Males steal, often with violence, the food females kill. When a new coalition takes over a pride, the males kill all the cubs. If a lioness won't mate with them, they may kill her, too. The females in a pride don't accept just any males, though. A takeover is successful only once a male or a coalition of males has proven to be strong enough to ensure the safety of the females and any cubs the new males may father.

Unless a lioness in breeding condition is available, a male seems to prefer the company of other males. When they are near a pride, the males sleep 10 to 20 yards away (9–18 m) from the closely packed females and cubs. But members of a coalition don't spend all of their time together. If they have a big territory, they may separate for days or even weeks so that each can patrol a portion. If one of the males encounters outsiders, the other members of his coalition hear his calls and come running to help defend their territory.

Lions on patrol check the females to see if any are ready to breed. They also warn off other males by marking the boundaries of their territory with urine and smelly chemicals from glands on their head. Male lions will not challenge trespassing females—only other males.

A coalition usually holds a pride for about 2 years before it is ousted by a younger, stronger, or bigger group. Large coalitions may stay in control of a pride for up to 4 years.

COMMUNICATION AND ROARING

Members of the cat family all make some similar sounds, but four can make an earsplitting sound that literally shakes the ground. The "four who can roar" are lions, leopards, tigers, and jaguars.

Lions roar the most and the loudest. The roar is, however, only one of a dozen calls these big cats use. They also communicate with physical gestures.

Making their intentions clear is important to group-living lions. Communication lessens the need to resort to violence. When lions approach other members of their pride or their coalition, they make a puffing sound that signals peaceable intentions. They also perform the lion greeting ceremony to show that they belong. The welcome consists of a soft moan and a head rub that mixes the two cats' scents and reinforces social bonds. The glands that have the marking scent are located on the chin, cheeks, and lips. The greeting is so enthusiastic that sometimes a lion is knocked right off its feet. The less powerful animal usually rubs the stronger one. Weaker males rub against stronger males, females rub against males, and cubs rub against adults.

A lion greeting

The talkative lions communicate in other ways as well. They meow, snarl, and make a sound similar to purring in order to express their needs to their companions. But when lions want to send long-distance messages, they roar. The mighty roar can be heard 5 or even 6 miles away (8–10 km).

Roaring is made possible by the two-piece **hyoid** bone in the throat. Cat species that can roar have a more flexible hyoid bone than cats that cannot. Lions can recognize the sound of other pride members' voices, and they roar to find each other if they are separated. Males generally have a deeper, louder roar than females.

Each roar lasts 30 or 40 seconds, but one call may follow another for an hour or more. Lions usually roar while standing or crouching, but it is possible to make the call from any position, even while running.

A true multipurpose call, roaring is most often used to claim a territory. It lets other lions know that a place is occupied and warns them not to trespass. To show that a pride is large and strong, all the members may roar together. Cubs add their tiny voices to the chorus of a roaring pride even though they can't make proper roars until they are 2 years old.

Roaring is usually heard when lions

Lions can tell the size of another pride by the number of voices they hear roaring.

are most active, the hours closest to dawn and dusk. Prides may roar a dozen times during a night. If one pride starts up, neighboring prides roar back. So strong is the urge to answer a roar that lions in the middle of a meal will stop eating to let loose the awesome sound.

THE LIFE OF A HUNTER

The lion is the top predator in its environment. A lion will eat a beetle or a giraffe—and most anything in between.

Lions have preferred prey, though. Their everyday diet consists of impala, waterbuck, zebra, and wildebeest, which are common species that are large enough to feed a group of hungry hunters yet not so big as to exhaust the hunters or endanger their lives.

Impalas (above), *weighing about 140 pounds (64 kg), and* warthogs (bottom left), *at about 175 pounds (80 kg), make quick meals for a pride of lions.* Wildebeests (left) *weigh about 450 pounds (205 kg) and are more substantial feasts.*

An adult male lion needs 5,600 pounds (2,500 kg) of meat every year. A lioness needs 4,000 pounds (1,800 kg). In order to get that much meat in a year, each lion must eat 15 to 35 animals the size of an antelope. Other carnivores such as bears or dogs have a digestive system that will allow them to live on berries and fruits when there is no meat, but cats don't. To survive, they must have meat.

If lions have access to water, they often drink after a large meal. In dry areas, lions can survive on the moisture they get from their prey.

Ten or more pounds of flesh is a satisfying meal for a lioness. Eating is not a series of regular meals, though. In hard times, lions might go days, even weeks, without eating. But when food is available, they stuff themselves. A hungry lioness may wolf down 20 percent of her body weight, socking away a 50-pound (23-kg) supper. That would be the equivalent of a fourth grader eating 100 hamburgers. A male lion might gobble up 80 pounds (36 kg) of meat. After one of their big feasts, lions don't need to hunt again for a week.

Lionesses travel about 3 miles (4.8 km) a day in search of food.

In hunting as in everything else, the pride has no leaders. But there are pride members who account for far more than their share of the kills.

Females do more than 90 percent of the hunting for a pride. Male lions can hunt for themselves, but they rarely make the effort if lionesses are nearby. The males usually wait for the females to make a kill and then steal the food from them. However, it takes a male coalition to overpower large game. Only males have the power it takes to tackle a giant giraffe or a heavyweight hippo.

When there are no lionesses to provide fresh meat, males sometimes rob other predators. The male lion's great strength makes it possible to steal from fellow carnivores such as leopards, cheetahs, jackals, hyenas, wild dogs, eagles, and vultures. Males might get as much as half of their food by stealing and **scavenging,** or feeding on dead animals that they find.

Hunting big animals involves injury and violent death—not always just for the prey. Lions are kicked, stabbed, trampled, and sometimes killed in their attempts to get food.

Lions are not very efficient killers. Only one in four attacks is successful. Lions often have trouble getting close enough to an animal to make a kill. Most antelopes and zebras can easily outrun them, so lions are forced to be sneaky. Creeping up on prey is called **stalking.** Hiding until prey comes close enough to be pounced on is called **ambushing.**

These are a lion's main hunting tactics.

A lion's chances of creeping up on prey are better when it is dark or almost dark, so lions usually sleep during the day and hunt by night.

In most hunts there is no plan. When the lionesses detect prey, they spread out and approach it from different directions. But they aren't truly cooperating. Each lioness is stalking on her own. Still, the presence of other hunters is useful. If a prey animal senses the approach of one of the lions, it might turn and run right into the path of another.

A lion has little chance of catching a wildebeest from this distance.

This prey animal, called a kudu, is probably safe from the attacking lioness. The lioness is changing direction to focus on another member of the herd.

In some prides the lionesses *are* a true team, hunting with well-thought-out tactics. This is, however, the exception rather than the rule. In these teams, younger members of the pride will often drive a herd of prey animals toward the more experienced hunters. A lioness, or more often a male lion, might deliberately show itself to frighten the prey, hoping it will run near one of the hidden hunters.

A charging lion can hit with enough force to knock down an animal two or three times heavier than itself. Sometimes this breaks the animal's neck and kills it instantly. But most animals weighing 100 to 200 pounds (45–90 kg) are killed by a spine-crushing bite to the back of the neck. Larger animals are either suffocated or strangled. When an animal is attacked by two lionesses, it might be suffocated by one and strangled by the other at the same time. To suffocate an animal, a lion puts its mouth over the nose of the prey until it dies from lack of oxygen. Strangulation is similar, but in this method the big cat grabs the underside of the animal's neck and bites down until the windpipe is crushed and the animal can't breathe. Surprisingly, most animals don't struggle once these holds are taken, and it is not unusual for the pride to begin eating while the victim is still alive.

Very large animals such as rhinos and hippos aren't easy to kill. They often die only after the lions claw and rip great chunks of flesh from their body.

Low rumbles of warning are followed by loud snarls and slapping paws as a pride devours a kill.

When an animal is killed, the meat is not shared equally. The strongest lions get the most to eat even if they have not helped with the hunting. They get it by force. In the crowded, frenzied effort to get a share, ears might get bitten off and eyes might be clawed out. In lion society, you have to be quick if you want to eat. Lions can devour an entire warthog in 5 minutes and a zebra carcass in 4 hours. One of the reasons for this speed-eating is competition from other animals. If the pride's resident males are nearby, they will trot up and drive off the lioness hunters. A pack of hyenas may also drive lionesses off a kill, but they too will turn tail when the male lions arrive.

Almost every part of an animal is eaten: skin, meat, intestines, eyeballs. Even the blood is lapped up. The first thing the pride eats is usually the contents of the intestines, which contain many important vitamins and minerals. The stomach, however, is discarded. It must smell bad to lions because they often bury it. If there is more meat than the lions can eat at once, they drag the carcass out of sight and stay close to guard it.

Scientists once thought that cooperative hunting was the main reason that lions lived in groups. They assumed that animals in big prides got more to eat than solitary hunters. Careful observations have shown, however, that a lioness hunting alone eats just as much, if not more, than the members of a large pride because she doesn't have to share her kills.

Lions sometimes hide carcasses in long grass or brush.

RAISING CUBS

At 3 or 4 years of age, a lioness becomes mature enough to have babies. Every 3 or 4 weeks, she comes into **estrus,** or the period in which she can become pregnant. During the 4 to 8 days of her estrus, she will mate every 15 or 20 minutes. A lioness may mate with more than one male during her estrus, so her **litter** may have cubs with different fathers. A lioness typically has a litter of 2 to 4 cubs every 2 years and gives birth to 10 to 15 cubs during her lifetime.

Lionesses do almost everything together, but they have their babies alone. When a lioness is close to the end of her 110-day pregnancy, she leaves the pride and goes to a **den,** a safe spot surrounded by thorn bushes or hidden away in some rocks. There she gives birth in secrecy to her cubs.

The newborn cubs are tiny—only about 2 pounds (0.9 kg)—and completely helpless. The lioness keeps her cubs hidden in the den, leaving them only to go hunting. When she is gone, which could be as long as 48 hours at a time, the babies stay quiet and still, even if they are very hungry. This is important to their survival. Predators such as hyenas and jackals will kill any unguarded lion cubs they find. Hiding is the only defense the cubs have. There are no teeth in the tiny carnivores' mouths until they are at least 3 weeks old. Lion cubs can't even see danger for a few days, because they are born with their eyes closed.

Young cubs need a good spot to hide from predators.

A cub's spots fade as it gets older—more quickly in males than females. Some lions retain faint spots even as adults.

A baby lion doesn't look much like its parents. Its gray hair is thick, woolly, and covered with spots. Its short, stumpy tail doesn't even have a tuft of black fur on the end.

Lion cubs grow rapidly, doubling their weight every week. By the time they are a month old, the cubs can walk well enough to travel with their mother and she rejoins the pride.

A lioness refuses to nurse a cub that is too old.

Lions have no special breeding season. Cubs are born throughout the year. However, all the females of a pride tend to give birth at about the same time. If a lioness dies, her cubs will be raised by the pride's other females. Although a lioness will give preference to her own cubs at feeding time, any cub is allowed to drink her milk.

You might think that the lionesses in a pride would take turns baby-sitting, but they usually do not. Most nights all the lionesses go hunting and leave the babies alone. Sometimes no adult comes back for a couple of days.

If the pride makes a kill nearby, one or more of the mothers will lead the cubs to the food. The tiniest babies can only lap up blood, but 3-month-old cubs have baby teeth and can chew on scraps of meat. When her cubs are about 6 months old, a mother lion stops producing milk. This is a very difficult time for the cubs because they are unable to hunt for themselves. Many young lions starve to death because cubs don't usually get a share of a kill until the adults are full.

Only one in five cubs will reach adulthood. There are a number of reasons for this. A mother may abandon young cubs if food is scarce and she grows too thin to feed them. Older cubs may starve because they are not able to compete successfully at kills. Disease, accidents, and other predators take a toll, too. But the greatest danger lion cubs face is a new coalition of adult male lions trying to take over a pride. If the attacking males are successful, they will kill or chase off the males from the old coalition and kill all their cubs. The death of the cubs causes the lionesses to come into estrus. The new lions then mate with them and father babies of their own. More than half of all cubs are killed by invading males. Lionesses vigorously defend their cubs against the males, but in one-on-one combat, they generally lose. However, if a pride has many lionesses and they fight together, they are sometimes successful in chasing off the murderous males. A lioness with cubs older than 6 months of age may save her babies by taking them away from the pride until they are independent. If a lioness with cubs trespasses on another pride's territory, though, the resident lionesses will attack her and her cubs.

Pridemates groom each other even as cubs.

Left and opposite: *Cubs practice hunting by attacking each other.*

Other kinds of cats learn to hunt by practicing, but lion cubs learn mainly by watching. Most of the animals that lions normally hunt are too big and dangerous for cubs to practice on. So they strengthen their muscles and sharpen their skills by pretending to hunt each other. Of course, if a grasshopper or frog hops into sight, it may get stalked.

At 10 months, youngsters are allowed to tag along when the lionesses hunt. Sometimes the cubs join in, more often than not ruining an ambush that took hours to set up. Cubs learn strategy and tactics by watching, but they can make a kill without benefit of experience or education. At 2 years of age, young lions can bring down prey as large as a gazelle by themselves.

At one year of age, male cubs get the first wisps of a mane, and they are larger in the head, shoulders, and chest than female cubs are.

When cubs reach their second birthday, it is a time for changes. Two-year-old females become full-fledged members of the pride, unless the pride has grown too large. In that case, young females go off on their own or with other females to form a new pride.

Males leave their birth pride when they are between 2 and 3 years of age. A few leave voluntarily, but most of the wispy-maned youngsters are driven off by the older males, who see these sexually mature males as challengers.

If he is lucky, an outcast will be accompanied by many same-age brothers and male cousins. **Nomads** such as these wander for several years as they grow strong enough to fight for a pride of females. A male lion becomes a nomad again after his coalition loses control of a pride.

Few wild male lions survive past 10 years of age. A lioness in the wild typically lives about 12 years. Captive lions, who don't have to fight or risk injury capturing prey, often live past 20.

LION TROUBLE

The trouble with lions is that the species is threatened with extinction. In Africa, where more than a million lions once roamed, fewer than one hundred thousand remain. In Asia, there are less than three hundred.

One reason there are fewer lions is because the number of people in Africa and Asia is increasing. More and more of the wild land is being turned into farms and ranches to support human families. The grasslands are being divided into small bits, which splits the lion population into small, isolated groups. Some scientists think this could lead to inbreeding, or mating of lions that are too closely related. This will be a future problem because inbred lions, like other inbred animals, are usually not very healthy.

When grassland is turned into farmland, some of the grazing animals that lions need for food starve to death or move to other areas. With less prey available, lions have less to eat. Soon there are fewer lions, too.

People who live on the newly developed land are frightened of the hungry lions and shoot or poison them to protect their families and livestock.

Human settlements have eaten up the wilderness where lions once roamed free.

Herds of wildebeests and zebras roam the grasslands of the Serengeti.

Most African countries have established national parks to preserve wildlife and wild places, but loggers, illegal hunters, and farmers trespass freely on them. Many of the countries are too poor to enforce the laws they have passed to protect the last of their wildlife.

Two large parks, Serengeti National Park in Tanzania and Kruger National Park in South Africa, are home to the two biggest populations of wild lions. The Serengeti National Park contains more than three thousand lions and encompasses 5,700 square miles (14,763 sq km), which is about the size of Connecticut. The Serengeti is surrounded by game reserves and other controlled areas. Lions are protected within the boundaries of the park, but hunting them is allowed in the game reserves. Researchers are studying the effect that hunting has on lion populations.

Covering 7,722 square miles (20,000 sq km), Kruger National Park is even bigger than the Serengeti. In Kruger and the private game parks that surround it, there are more than two thousand lions. Illegal hunting is a problem, so Kruger has many rangers to protect the animals.

Asiatic lions are in much greater danger of extinction than African lions are.

The Gir forest in India is the last place where there are wild Asiatic lions. The forest is divided into two areas, a national park that is just for wild animals, and a wildlife sanctuary where people and their livestock also live. Together they form the Gir Protected Area, which covers about 545 square miles (1,412 sq km)—about half the size of Rhode Island.

Sometimes lions in Gir kill livestock because it is easier than finding other prey. The herdsmen then try to kill the lions. The Indian government has tried several methods to save the lions. The authorities pay farmers for cows and sheep that are killed by lions, but the farmers are still angry. The government has also tried moving people away from the park. That hasn't been very successful either.

The situation is getting worse because the lion population is starting to outgrow the sanctuary. Since the early 1990s, 30 to 40 lions have claimed territories outside of Gir. The Indian government is planning to relocate some of the lions to another protected area. Splitting the population would reduce some of the pressures on the Gir Protected Area and would protect the Asiatic lions against extinction if a disease or natural disaster should hit Gir.

Even within highly maintained parks, lions are vulnerable to threats such as disease. In 1994, about one-third of the lions in the Serengeti died of a disease called distemper. The disease came from pet dogs living in villages around the park. Dogs transmitted distemper to predators such as wild dogs and hyenas, who passed it on to lions, probably while fighting over food. There is a vaccine that will prevent this disease, but scientists knew it would be impossible to give all of the lions a shot! Instead, they began to vaccinate the dogs that lived in villages near the park. By 1998, more than half the dogs from the targeted areas had been vaccinated and the number of lions in the Serengeti had nearly returned to what it was before the distemper epidemic started.

Domesticated dogs (above) *and Cape buffalo* (bottom left) *have brought disease to lion populations in Africa.*

Disease has also affected lions in Kruger National Park. One of the Kruger lions' favorite foods, the Cape buffalo, often carries a disease called tuberculosis. Lions who eat sick buffalo usually get the disease and die from it. The South African government is trying to stop the tuberculosis, which spread to the buffalo from cattle that live around the park, but they have not been very successful. In 1999, an outbreak of a fatal bacterial disease called anthrax killed prey animals and the lions that ate them.

One of the best hopes for lions is private land in the hands of conservationists. The lions in this book were photographed at such a place, the Rattray family's Mala Mala Game Reserve on the edge of the Kruger National Park. Mala Mala is the largest privately owned game reserve in South Africa. The only hunting allowed there is with a camera and binoculars. The grasslands and forests of Mala Mala support more than 200 species of wildlife, including lions. There, more than 50 of the big cats live as wild and free as the African winds. In this special sanctuary we came to care about lions and hope that when you have read our book, you will care about them, too.

GLOSSARY

ambushing: hiding in order to attack by surprise

canines: long, sharp teeth used to inflict stabbing bites

carnassials: sharp teeth in the cheek area used to slice meat from a carcass

carnivores: animals that eat meat

coalitions: groups of male lions that band together for strength

cubs: baby lions

den: a sheltered spot used by a lioness to hide her newborn cubs

estrus: the period during which a female animal is able to become pregnant

hyoid: a u-shaped bone or series of bones at the back of the throat that supports the muscles of the tongue and allows lions to roar

keratin: a protein that is found in human fingernails and lions' claws

litter: a group of baby animals born at the same time to one mother

mammals: animals that produce milk to feed their young

mane: long fur that grows on the neck and shoulders of a male lion

nomads: male lions that have no fixed home and wander from place to place in search of food

papillae: small, backward-pointing hooks on the top of a lion's tongue

predators: animals that hunt other animals for food

prey: animals that are hunted for food

pride: a group of female lions that live and hunt together

scavenging: feeding on animals that are already dead, rather than hunting live animals

stalking: creeping up on an animal

tapetum lucidum: a layer of reflective cells at the back of a lion's eye that allows it to see better in low-light conditions

territory: an area that is occupied by a group of lions and is defended from other lions

INDEX

ABOUT THE AUTHOR AND PHOTOGRAPHER

Kathy Darling (top) and **Tara Darling-Lyon** (bottom) are a mother/daughter team who specialize in writing about animals. Kathy, the mother, does the writing and Tara takes the photographs for their books about endangered and threatened species. Together they have produced over 30 books, many of them prizewinners. Their writing projects have taken them to Tasmania, Mongolia's Gobi desert, Indonesia's Komodo island, South Africa, the Amazon, the Arctic, and many other exciting places.

Kathy began her career as an editor and has written more than 100 books for kids, including hands-on science and storybooks. Tara was an otter and penguin keeper and trained seals before becoming a full-time animal photographer.

Both Kathy and Tara raise dogs as a hobby. Tara has Irish water spaniels and Kathy has Irish wolfhounds. They live in Larchmont, New York.

Additional photographs are reproduced through the courtesy of: © Aaron Ferster/Photo Researchers, Inc., p. 8 (bottom left); © François Gohier/Photo Researchers, Inc., p. 8 (center and top left); © Mitch Reardon/Photo Researchers, Inc., p. 27; © Mark Boulton/Photo Researchers, Inc., p. 39; © M. P. Kahl/Photo Researchers, Inc., pp. 40–41; © E. Hanumantha Rao/Photo Researchers, Inc., p. 42; © Michele Burgess, p. 43. Illustration on p. 9 by Laura Westlund, © Carolrhoda Books, Inc.